CW01023511

Hair/Power

Published by 404 Ink Limited
www.404Ink.com
@404Ink

All rights reserved © Kajal Odedra, 2023.

The right of Kajal Odedra to be identified as the Author of this
Work has been asserted by her in accordance with the
Copyright, Designs and Patent Act 1988.

No part of this publication may be reproduced, distributed, or transmitted,
in any form or by any means, electronic, mechanical, photocopying, recording,
or otherwise, without first obtaining the written permission of the rights
owner, except for the use of brief quotations in reviews.

Please note: Some references include URLs which may change or be unavailable
after publication of this book. All references within endnotes were accessible
and accurate as of February 2023 but may experience link rot from there on in.

Editing & typesetting: Laura Jones
Cover design: Luke Bird
Co-founders and publishers of 404 Ink:
Heather McDaid & Laura Jones

Print ISBN: 978-1-912489-70-1
Ebook ISBN: 978-1-912489-71-8

Printed and bound in Great Britain by Clays Ltd, Elcograf S.p.A.

Hair/Power

Essays on Control and Freedom

Kajal Odedra

Inklings

Contents

For the Odedra girls

Prologue

When I started to think about hair and its power, I didn't know where to start. It is a messy, tangled subject. It is vast yet so personal. It is dominating yet we don't quite realise the impact it has. While ruminating over this, I read Susan Sontag's 1979 diaries where she reflects on the allure of lists.

'I perceive value, I confer value, I create value, I even create – or guarantee – existence. Hence, my compulsion to make "lists." The things (Beethoven's music, movies, business firms) won't exist unless I signify my interest in them by at least noting down their names.'[1]

A decade later, in the same diaries, she writes a list of all her likes (fires, Venice, tequila, sunsets, babies, silent films) and dislikes (washing her hair (or having it washed)).

Sontag railed against the standards placed on women and wrote extensively about beauty, sexuality and power. It seems comforting to me, when in the face of messy, complicated matters so entwined in every inch of our lives, to create some order with a list. Her lists were a way of examining, a place to begin. Perhaps to see something objectively, we need to start by listing all of the things, like they are objects?

So, in a nod to Sontag, here is a list of my dislikes and likes about hair:

Things I dislike
My moustache,
The hair on the sides of my face (though sometimes I am endeared by it),
The maintenance of being a woman with a lot of hair,
Cutting myself when I shave,
Malting in every house I live or rest in,
Razors,
Bleach,
My hairy fingers,
In-grown hairs,
Hair found in food,
Hair found in my mouth.

<u>Things I like</u>
The colour of my hair that fools people into thinking it's
    black when it's really dark brown,
The smell of myself when I have hairy armpits and don't
    wear deodorant,
The feeling of shaving months old hair from my legs,
Using a strand of hair as substitute for floss,
How free I feel when I don't shave at all,
Tweezing (any part of my body),
Playing with other people's hair,
My hairy arms,
Unearthing an ingrown hair,
Having my hair pulled and played,
Washing my hair (or having it washed).

Introduction

When my mum first allowed me to bleach my moustache I was convinced my life was about to change. I was fourteen and had waited a long time for this moment, of removing the obstacle I saw in my path to being accepted. I imagined the boy in my class who I had a crush on asking me out. I imagined the pretty girls finally wanting to be my friend, the girls without black whiskers growing on their upper lips. My life was about to really begin.

The bleach I had waited for all this time came in a turquoise and white tub, it was called Jolen. Just like the one I had seen my sister use over the years but Mum had refused to let me until I was 'old enough'.

I opened the tub of thick white cream, dense and heavy, smelling of dangerous chemicals, reassuring its ability to solve my problems. It came with a tube of powder that I carefully measured out into a saucer with the accompanying plastic measuring spoon. I added dollops of the thick cream and mixed until it was a paste that held so much hope. My sister did this very ritual every few weeks like a student preparing for an exam. I applied it thickly, covering every sprinkling of hair above my top lip. It stung almost immediately. *But that's a good sign*, I thought, *it must be working.* Sat on the edge of my bed, eyes glued to the clock for ten minutes before scrambling into the bathroom. Still reading the instructions to make sure I completed every step to the letter, I carefully wiped away the cream using wet toilet paper. I could feel a burn with every touch and washed my upper lip in cold water to cool it down. I dabbed it dry, careful not to aggravate my now very pink and tender skin. I looked in the mirror, expecting, hoping, it had vanished. But I could still see it. Clearly. Except now my moustache was a yellow that didn't quite blend in with my brown skin. Worse, it seemed to glow, drawing more attention to itself. *Maybe it will get better when the area is less red.* It didn't. School the next day was excruciating. I felt humiliated as I pretended not to hear the sniggers and, at times, blatant laughter in my face. After a few tries in later months, I got the hang of bleaching to the correct shade. And a few years later I was allowed to graduate to hair removal cream.

I've been a bit obsessed with hair all my life. Partly because I am a hairy person, more so than your average white girl

6

at least, but I'm probably averagely hairy for an Indian. When I was young, that didn't matter because the world I existed in for most of my childhood was white. The books were white, the people on TV were white, and the kids at school, so white. I wanted to be like them all. For a long time I went to great lengths to contort myself as much as I could. I shaved everything including my arms because they were abhorrently hairy to me. I dyed my hair blonde. I over-tweezed my already thin eyebrows. I tried to hide my Indian identity. I felt ashamed when people asked me about it. I felt I was a lower class just from my brown skin and Indian heritage. Rather than feeling proud of the hard work, long hours and many obstacles my parents had to overcome to get me to the white school, the white university, I felt I should to hide it, so that people might assume I was like them. I was so dissociated from myself it was like acting in a play but without a script, winging it, hoping nobody noticed I wasn't supposed to be there.

It wasn't until my mid-twenties, while I worked as an activist, that I realised how much hate I'd internalised. Campaigning with young people and refugees became my day job while I volunteered in the evenings and weekends. I became conscious of the power dynamics I existed in, not just politically but also the way I perceived my own body, the way I existed in spaces. That power dynamics were playing out *everywhere*.

Michel Foucault, mid-20th century French philosopher, said there is no knowledge that isn't influenced by power. That power is constituted through accepted forms of knowledge, scientific understanding and our ideas of 'truth'. Politics and 'regimes of truth' are the result of scientific discourse and institutions, and are reinforced (and redefined) constantly through the education system, the media, and the flux of political and economic ideologies. In this sense, the 'battle for truth' is not for some absolute truth that can be discovered and accepted, but is a battle about 'the rules according to which the true and false are separated and specific effects of power are attached to the true.'[1] Science, history, art, nothing is objectively true, the knowledge we consume is power at play.

Everything I learned and understood about myself was subjective to the space and time I occupied. There was no objective truth about my appearance and whether I belonged. Disillusioned, I was frustrated with having soaked up all that nonsense for so long. For only starting to question it in my adulthood.

I embraced myself, stopped shaving my arms. I don't know how but when the hair grew back I no longer felt ashamed. Returning home from London for weekends I learned about my heritage and was so curious. I would ask my parents questions about when they first arrived to the UK, what was it like for them? What did they struggle with? I wanted to know my mum's recipes – I would stand by the hob while she poured spices into her creations, irritating her by asking for specific measurements. *Just a bit, whatever you think. We don't measure!*

Foucault believed that our ways of thinking were limited by the knowledge of the day, and that stopped us from growing. I wanted to write the essays in *Hair/Power* to analyse how the knowledge and perceptions we have about hair is shackling our freedom. This book is not a history of hair, nor is it a thesis – I'm not going to tell you what to think or what to do after reading.

The word 'essay' derives from the French 'essayer', meaning 'to try' or 'to attempt'. Michel de Montaigne was the first author to describe his work as essays, in the 16th century, to say that he was attempting to put his thoughts into writing.[2] In the coming pages I offer such essays that explore how hair has impacted me, as well as other identities and cultures, but I can't claim to be speaking from any experience and lens other than my own.

So this is a 'try' at hair; a contemplation, an enquiry, an excavation. It is a conversation with Foucault and Sontag and my childhood. A complicated love letter. Hair, that is so wrapped up in my sense of self and intrinsic to my path into activism. This is a try at what hair means to me.

Chapter 1
Blondes/Conformity

Stacey's hair was golden. She had a fringe that would flirt with the lashes of her eyes. When she looked up it was like she was peering through a curtain. In all the books in our primary school library, the characters looked like Stacey. Perfectly blonde, perfectly blue-eyed. They were often very kind and ingratiating. The perfect little girls. Stacey wasn't always kind. In fact, she could be quite cruel, in the way girls learn to be on the playground. The other girls didn't compare to Stacey, but they were in her chorus. Each week she would pick her favourite, the chosen girl who would be allowed to bathe in Stacey's limelight, have the privilege of walking hand in hand, promenading the concrete playground. She would sit with Stacey at registration and sometimes be invited to her home for fish fingers, if she was lucky.

I was not like Stacey. In fact, I could be deemed her exact opposite. My hair was so dark that the other kids would say it's black. *It's dark brown, look!* I'd protest while placing the strands against a black surface to expose its lighter colour, because I didn't want to be associated with the word 'Black'. It was incongruous to the world I lived in then. My world before was a safe bubble in Leicester, where the kids looked like me and talked like my family, with dark skin and thick accents from different parts of the world. Now I was in Newhall, an ex-mining village in Derbyshire, and I didn't look, or sound, like anyone around there. Everything was white.

It is suffocating to feel constantly at the mercy of those around you. A relentless rebound, from one person's expectations to another. I thought it was just the kids at school that made me feel I had to be a particular way, to fit into the whiteness, but I realise now it was coming from every direction. It was pouring out of the libraries, TV screens, the subtle nods of approval and frowns of disapproval from adults telling us what is the right and wrong way to be. It was coming from our school corridors, from the teachers, the governors, the local authorities, the rules they all imposed.

There is a well-known adage, 'Children do not do what we say, they do what we do.'[1] They are primed to conform like balls of playdough, doing their best to live up to the rules and norms they are fed. Some children walk an even higher tightrope, an act in balancing not only the expectations of one culture and society they live in, but two; their home community (the society they live in) and their diaspora community (those from their homeland).

Studies into diaspora communities have identified the idea of cultural homelessness for those who have migrated to a new context, a 'unique experience and feeling reported by some multicultural individuals' who are torn between identifying with the different cultures they are in, and are not sure what place to call 'home'. Sometimes individuals in these groups will choose to identify with one group versus another. As a second generation immigrant, it took me a while to pick a side, I was in a passionate limbo with both cultures. When my family and I lived in Leicester, I was initially fully immersed in my Indian community and culture, with its large Asian community. I wanted to be like my older sister and cousins, to fit into that world. But it didn't take long after moving to Derbyshire when I was seven, for me to put the white culture I was then in on a pedestal.

Whether we assimilate or not, it is impossible not to be influenced by a new environment. Some hold their heritage tighter, becoming more traditional, more religious in the transition. In other examples, the new culture will mix in with the primary, creating a new, third culture. But there is no going back to what the immigrants had, back in their home country, where they have just one culture to tackle. Once a person immigrates, they are changed forever. This whole experience can be even harder for the children born into a diaspora, who are encountering the two cultures either simultaneously or in close succession, a balancing act that no one can prepare them for. I soon found myself vying for the contradictory approval of the white kids at school and the Indian community at home. At once craving to appear more white and be accepted as a 'Good Indian Girl'.

My mum grew my hair long and tended to it like it was a prized garden. She kept it shiny and strong with a weekly treatment of coconut oil. She plaited and decorated it in colourful scrunchies, ribbons and decorative flowers. My hair wasn't my own, not yet. It was hers. And it was my auntie's and grandma's and God's. On Sunday evenings I sat down at my mum's feet, who methodically combed my mane, both of us lost in this ritual. For school she plaited it in all kinds of complicated styles, braids criss-crossing my head in different directions, my hair pulled so tight it stretched back the skin on my face. My hair was so long it was a creature with a life of its own. My sisters too, all four of us, had long, dark silky hair that was forbidden to be tampered with. No fringe, no short haircuts. Stacey's blonde fringe cut across her forehead in a block. It was textured, heavy and thick. She had hair to die for. Our hair had to stay pure and uncut like the Good Indian Girls we were.

I spent my life straddling an Indian community where long hair was shorthand for beauty, docility, and fertility. The perfect woman. You can see it everywhere, from the copies of classical Rajput paintings in my auntie's home to Bollywood films I watched with my grandma, the movie star floating across the screen with black hair in a long plait falling across her sari. The opposite of that was in the films too, the woman with 'open' (loose) hair, blowing in the wind, as the vixen, the temptress.

One day, I was picked to play with Stacey at lunchtime, but it wasn't as fun as it seemed from afar. She was showing off in front of the boys and making me feel small. She was using me to entertain. She asked about my hair, *It's always in plaits*. It felt like an accusation. I said that I had it down on the weekends, which wasn't true but I would have said anything to seem normal in that moment. *How long is it?* I say that it's long, so long I can sit on it. Suspicious, she looked at me like I was a liar so to prove it I pulled apart the tightly woven plaits that my mum had braided that morning. The rush of fitting in, of impressing, I couldn't help it, it was intoxicating. Stacey blinked, unimpressed, and turned her attention to the next shiny thing.

When she picked me up, my mum's face dropped as though I had turned up in the playground undressed, mortified at my loose hair, untamed from its plaits. I felt sexualised through her shameful gaze. Her disappointment, her disgust, was hard to bear and something that would stay with me.

What I didn't quite understand then was how hard life was for my parents. A minefield to move to a new country with a radically different culture, then to have children in that context. The pressure to hold on to their heritage and what they had learned to be good and right, fighting against a tide that their children were immersed in. There is a fear of losing what you came with, your identity, the very core of who you are.

Like that day in school, I was always playing two characters. Double-cast in a performance, made to rush on and off stage, swapping my costume and make-up as fast as I could. I picked up tricks along the way. I had to think fast on my feet if someone asked a question at school that stumped me (*Where are you going on holiday this summer?*) because I didn't have the same life that they led (we didn't go on summer holidays, at best we went to Leicester to see my gran), so I learned to lie (I once said I was going to Hawaii... sometimes my lies were outrageous). This double-identity can also happen to kids who aren't in a diaspora, for those who are indigenous but, through time, have been marginalised in their own country.

*

Jakobe Sanden was seven years old when he was pulled out of class in his Utah school and sent home.[2] Jakobe's school picture from 2015 shows him kneeling, his palm resting on his right knee, beaming with pride and a toothy grin. He has a mohawk, a traditional haircut among many Native American groups, including the Seneca Nation that he was part of. The school Jakobe attended had a dress code that read, 'students have the responsibility to avoid grooming that causes a distraction or disruption, interrupting school decorum and adversely affecting the educational process.' Jakobe's parents were told that day that their son's hair would be a 'distraction' and they had to get it cut or leave the school. Reports about the incident detailed how confused Jakobe was and his parents hurt. Like my parents, they had spent their lives trying to juggle their culture with the country they lived in. The difference was they hadn't migrated to the US, the country they lived in *was* their homeland.

The Native American Nations are also known as the First Nations, having occupied what is now known as the United States at least 15,000 years ago. Subsequent European colonisation led to a war waged on this native population, resulting in massacres and forced assimilation for those left behind. Though there are now 574 federally recognised tribes living in the country, they have fought against the odds to gain their rights. In 2009, an 'apology to Native Peoples of the United States' was included in the Defense Appropriations Act. It stated that the US apologised for 'the many instances of violence, maltreatment, and neglect inflicted on Native Peoples by citizens of the United States.'[3]

Jakobe's story is one of so many where the invisible rules we abide by come into plain sight. The irony is that the rules are not so old or ancient that they are protected from fresh scrutiny. The Seneca culture precedes the European culture that broadly replaced it across the United States. The act of policing traditions thousands of years older than the body that's governing is beyond arrogant. It's dehumanising.

Our cultures; the traditions within them, the markers that we adopt to express who we are, what we value, what we believe in, are instinctive and develop through generations. As tribal creatures, we need them to bind us, to maintain connection. Tradition helps us achieve a sense of inner peace and self-acceptance, feeling grounded in our core identity.[4] When those traditions are disregarded, it can feel like an existential rejection.

During the episode in Utah, the Seneca Nation Tribal Councillor William Canella wrote to the school district superintendent: 'From past centuries to the modern era, Native [American] boys have worn their hair in various lengths and styles to demonstrate their pride in their heritage... It is common for Seneca boys to wear a Mohawk, because after years of discrimination and oppression, they are proud to share who they are.'[5]

Following a media uproar, Jakobe was eventually allowed back to school and to keep his haircut. But he was also given a clear unspoken message, that his identity and how he expressed it would be up for discussion throughout his life. That, unlike his fellow classmates, he wasn't free to bloom without repercussions. His growth would happen in extremes, under a microscope or in the dark. Policed or pushed off stage.

How we feel about our body depends on our context. I didn't notice my body hair until it was pointed out to me, in the way that you wouldn't really notice the creases of your palm or the pink of your tongue unless someone had something to say about it. An innocuous body part that you neither like nor deplore. The hair on my face and toes. My arms and legs. I could have gone on blissfully for a good number of years without giving it a second thought if I'd been surrounded by people who had the same skin and hair as me. The beauty of assimilation is that everyone who fits in feels neither special nor like a freak. It's what you dream of, as a child who doesn't fit in, to be invisible. But the girls at my school didn't have any unwanted hair. They would glow with their blonde so fine, so discreet, it lay on their pale limbs like a golden sheen. It looked almost angelic.

I felt so abnormal that when I was a young teen I secretly went to my family doctor to get tested for poly-cystic ovary syndrome (PCOS), a hormonal condition in some women that can cause serious issues including enlarged ovaries and cysts, but I'd also heard how a person with PCOS can have an unusual abundance of hair as well as weight gain and acne. I didn't have any of those other symptoms but I was obsessed with my hair and convinced myself there was a bigger problem. Maybe I hoped there was a medical issue to blame because there would be a solution other than the one I had – to face a lifetime of removing it.

What I realise now is that almost all women have hairy arms and facial whiskers, some are just more obvious than others. I was unfortunate to spend my formative years among a dominant identity that wasn't my own. When I looked into Mediterranean, Asian and Middle Eastern cultures, I found women like me. In her book, *Women with Moustaches, Men Without Beards*, Afsaneh Najmabadi explores how ideas of male and female beauty in Iran under the Qajar dynasty in 1785 – 1925 were more similar to one another. She writes that sexuality and sexual identity was more fluid, with facial hair and femininity presented in both genders, lovers in portraits indistinguishable in their gender if it wasn't for their clothing. It wasn't until Europe began to influence Iranian society through travel and trade that these ideals slowly changed.[6] Najmabadi has spoken about how her research of this period in history changed dramatically after she looked up from historical texts and viewed the art of the time. The paintings revealed an entire world of that period that hadn't been recorded in text, perhaps because of Europe's dominance and influence in how that history was documented. But underneath the colonial gaze was the reality, the secrets for how our bodies could be free.

Chapter 2
Buzz Cuts/Anger

When I was eight or nine years old, I plucked my eyelashes. I can't remember how it started, but I knew instinctively it was something I should hide. I'd do it secretly in the queue for school dinners, looking down at the floor while I tugged at my lids, or in the privacy of my bed at night.

I was an uncomfortable kid and felt like life was happening *to* me. I was told what to wear, how to have my hair, what was cool. I tried so hard to be like the kids at school. I manufactured a passion for horses, even though I'd never so much as laid eyes on a real horse in my life, just because that's what some of my friends at school were into (and they actually went horse riding). I experienced an added layer of submission as an Indian kid from a traditional family. I was told, in discreet (and sometimes not so discreet) ways, how to behave like a girl, that I shouldn't get too close to the boys, how the rules I lived by were different to the others at school. There was no option but to obey. It also felt like life was happening *to* my family. The regular racist abuse we endured in the Derbyshire village, the silence from authorities when my family turned to them for help, be it police, teachers, the council. The events around us seemed to be out of our hands, no matter what we did, the outcome would be the same. So I'd pluck at my hair, maybe an attempt to feel control and keep my anger under the surface.

Years later, I was going through a difficult time in my twenties, struggling with an intensity of depression and anxiety that I'd never experienced before. I needed to do something to deal with it. It was new year's eve and I was feeling desperate about my year ahead. I decided to go to a salon for an extreme hair cut, bringing my sister for courage. My hair was long, touching the top of my waist. Almost always this length, it was a big part of my identity. I asked the hairdresser to cut it to my chin, to chop away at my sense of self. Self-inflicted penance. The hairdresser took my hair in his hands, both of us looking in the mirror. 'So to here?' he asked, pointing the scissors below my shoulders. 'No, higher.' He lifted it an inch 'higher'. Turning to my sister he nervously asked, 'Is she sure about this?' In his profession he had probably had one too many customers like this, on the edge, in some kind of unspoken turmoil, asking him to be complicit in their unravelling. I eventually won the tug of war and pushed him to cut my hair as I asked. It was *very* short. As I left the salon I felt high, almost euphoric. I had walked into that place deeply sad and hopeless and something changed. I left feeling momentarily free.

In both of these instances, decades apart, I used my hair as a coping mechanism for dealing with an inner rage. Why, when we are emotionally heightened, do we reach for our hair? Is it self-harm? To do something within our control, change something, mutilate something? Each time I did it, I felt satiated. Maybe even stronger as I returned to face my world anew.

Anger is the awkward child in the playground, unsure where it belongs. As a primal emotion it once saved our lives, preparing us for fight or flight. The problem is that in our modern world, it's less useful to be sent into a jolt of panic. The danger our body typically detects is no longer the life-or-death situation that it once perceived. Our contexts have changed but our bodies haven't caught up. Anger still prepares us for a mythical battle. It prepared me when I stood in line at school, plucking away at my eyelashes, anxious and frustrated in my little world, doing what I could to fight, to fly. When I walked into that salon feeling like I needed to arm up, to face what I was going through with a sword and shield, cutting my hair so drastically made me imagine going into war, a soldier being prepared with a buzz cut.

Buzz cuts are a rite of passage in joining the US military, dating back to George Washington's leadership of the Continental Army. In the UK, it's up to the commander. The reason for them, initially, was hygiene, to stem the spread lice in the field. Since then, other benefits have been found, including the belief that uniformity creates obedience, critical in a military context. But until recently, though they were allowed in the army, women were not allowed to get a buzz cut. There were military regulations in some branches of the US Army that stated women must keep their hair a certain length, 'hair cannot protrude past the bottom of the collar and the fringe can't reach below the eyebrows.'[1] A shaved head was considered 'eccentric or faddish' for women and banned. In reality this was another way to control women, dividing the force into two categories, one of them the 'real soldiers' who were given the buzz cuts. We simply cannot cope with women breaking the mould of what they are expected to do. We need only to look at the incident with Jada Pinkett Smith at the 2022 Oscars ceremony to see further proof. Pinkett-Smith, who had recently adopted a shaved head because of her alopecia, was the butt of a joke by the host Chris Rock. Typical for a Hollywood awards ceremony, the joke was barely funny, low-hanging fruit. 'Jada, I love you. *G.I. Jane 2*, can't wait to see it.' Soon, her partner, Will Smith, strode on stage and slapped Rock across the face before going back to his seat, shouting for Rock to keep his wife's name out of his mouth. A lot was made of this moment in the press and general media, in the hours, days, months after. I'm sure it will be referenced for years. But what was striking to me was how little of Pinkett-Smith, who was at the centre of the incident, was a part of the discussion. How is it that a woman shaving her head can lead to such an intense media circus in 2022? And still, she is side-lined from the debate. All of the commentary was on the men, whether the joke was acceptable, what the consequences for comedians should be, how we as audiences judge Black men, what it will mean for Smith's reputation, etc. Very few seemed to be asking how the woman at the centre felt, what it was like to have alopecia in the public eye, whether the global attention on her appearance was warranted.

That is by no means the first time we have experienced a global frenzy because a female celebrity shaved her head. In 2007, when mega star Britney Spears was photographed by paparazzi giving herself a buzz cut, it sent shock waves across the media. It was one of the most subversive acts a pop star had done in decades. Why did it cause such interest and uproar? Why does society need women to have hair on their head? Why, when hair is removed, is society offended on a mass scale? And Spears wasn't just any woman, this was the former pop princess whom the media and public felt a level of ownership of from the age of 16, younger if you count her days as part of The Mickey Mouse Club in the early '90s.

At the time of her drastic haircut, she had been going through what seemed like a very public breakdown, amidst a divorce and a custody battle for her children. When she walked into the salon with her bodyguard, she asked the hairdresser to shave it all off. When the hairdresser asked why, Spears apparently said 'I just don't want anybody touching my head. I don't want anyone touching my hair. I'm sick of people touching my hair.' When the hairdresser refused, Spears took the clippers and started to shave it herself. According to the hairdresser, Esther Tognozz, Spears showed little emotion as she did it, except for tears in her eyes and voicing fear for her mother's reaction when she looked at her newly shorn head in the mirror.[2]

We now know that this was a precursor to the subsequent conservatorship that was placed on Spears, giving her father entire control over her life and business, removing most of Spears's freedom. Fifteen years later, I look at this moment and I see a woman fighting back. Spears had been controlled for her entire life even before the conservatorship. Apparently when she sat at the salon she spoke about the hair extensions they put on her for performing being too tight on her head but her complaints were ignored. She wanted it all to stop but she had no voice and so she acted out to be heard, doing the thing that seemed the most outrageous. Not just because it would impact her career as a bubble gum pop star, but because as a woman it was deemed highly inappropriate. Spears was in battle with her identity, defending herself by removing a part of herself from public scrutiny and reach.

It was also a sign of an angry woman and that is something current Western society cannot abide. Christianity and the Bible, intricately intertwined in Western culture, view anger as a flaw, a vengeful trait. 'Refrain from anger, and forsake wrath! Fret not yourself; it tends only to evil.'[3] And the feeling of anger is wrapped up in guilt and remorse. Worse, it is shameful. It's implied that anger is the opposite of love, 'But you, O Lord, are a God merciful and gracious, slow to anger and abounding in steadfast love and faithfulness.'[4] Spears's actions were shamed by practically every media outlet. Journalists went to psychiatrists for comment, quick to diagnose Spears of mental illness, of going 'crazy'. In his essay, 'On Anger', the Stoic philosopher Seneca asserted, in the first century CE, that anger is a temporary madness, and that even when justified, we should never act on the basis of it.

'[While] Other vices affect our judgement, anger affects our sanity: others come in mild attacks and grow unnoticed, but men's minds plunge abruptly into anger. There is no passion that is more frantic, more destructive to its own self; it is arrogant if successful, and frantic if it fails. Even when defeated it does not grow weary, but if chance places its foe beyond its reach, it turns its teeth against itself.'[5]

Rage can be suppressed for so long, that eventually when it is let out, it explodes. Mahsa Amini, from Iran's Kurdistan Province, was arrested on 13 September 2022 while visiting her uncle in Tehran with her family. While with her brother, wearing a hijab as the local rules dictated, Amini was pulled aside by Iran's Morality Police, a special force designated to ensure the people of Iran obey its rules to 'protect virtue and prevent vice.' Some say she was told her trousers were too tight, others that her veil was too loose. The authorities call both 'bad hijab', the inappropriate dress of a woman. Her brother tried to intervene, explaining that they weren't familiar with the specific rules of Tehran, but she was arrested and held for a one-hour 'briefing.' She never left that briefing, though her brother waited outside for as long as he could. Three days later, she was taken to the hospital in a stretcher. Amini died in hospital with multiple blows to the head, according to reporters. Her family say she was beaten to death but the police reject the allegations, saying Amini died after being taken to a hospital because she had a heart attack.[6]

She was a shy and reserved woman who never challenged the country's clerical rulers or its Islamic dress code, sources close to the family have said. Her death has sparked rage among the women of Iran and around the world, who have taken to the streets to remove their hijabs in public, some even burning them. The protests escalated, strikingly, to women cutting their hair in protest of the Islamic laws of Iran. They chanted 'Woman! Life! Freedom!' Riot police responded with pellet guns and water cannons, killing hundreds of protesters on the streets. 'We want to show them that we don't care about their standards, their definition of beauty or what they think that we should look like,' said thirty-six-year-old Faezeh Afshan, an Iranian chemical engineer living in Bologna, Italy, who was filmed shaving off her hair. 'It is to show that we are angry.'[7]

The movement these women are leading has the energy of a revolution. The courage and audacity to remove the hijab, to burn the hijab, to cut off one's hair. Cutting my own hair was low stakes for me, I had little to lose. It is the opposite for these women. To break the Islamic laws of their country and to deign taking to the streets and call the authorities to account is serious disobedience. But these women are raging. That anger is making headlines and it could quite possibly lead to a regime change.

The pressure to keep anger at bay or, at the very, to keep it hidden, ratchets up for those of us on the margins. But in the last few decades we have seen more and more women kicking back at the expectations placed on them, often leading the way for change. In her book, *Rage Becomes Her: The Power of Women's Anger*, writer and activist Soraya Chemaly says, 'Today, we see girls and women at the forefront of movements fighting for climate change and resisting authoritarianism. They are demanding an end to institutional tolerance of corruption, sexual violence and discrimination. They are, significantly, taking the risks that come with the open, public and political claim to anger.'[8]

A person's ability to 'control oneself' has been accepted as a virtue without question in Western society. But what if we took a different look at anger, and perceived what these women are doing, what Britney Spears was doing, as essential? That the only way to express themselves truly, purely, loudly, was to take to their hair? That sacred thing typically only lost through disease and age. The fact that a woman would choose to do this is testimony to her strength of feeling. So shouldn't we listen to what she has to say?

I used to think of my emotions, my ability to be messy in my joy and fierce in my conviction, as my superpower. The working class environment I grew up in held the concept of a strong character in high esteem. The boys and girls at school who got ahead were opinionated and bolshy. Wallflowers didn't get a look in. I learned to survive in that environment by telling jokes fast and slamming down bullies when I had the guts. When we were old enough to start going on nights out, it wasn't uncommon for a girlfriend to throw a drink in someone's face or for a fight to break out on the dance floor. My family, too, with their Indian fiery temperament, embraced passion, slamming doors and screaming matches. Arriving at university, these strong emotions were challenged. The people I studied with were broadly from better-off families and education. I was often mocked for sounding 'common' and tried to fit in by observing and adapting, much in the way I observed and adapted when my family first moved to Newhall. The student population at my university was largely from private or boarding school education, people who might be described as 'well bred' by some, and 'toffs' by others. I learned that the rules in my hometown were specific to that community. Here, it would take different behaviour to get by. Since then, I've occupied spaces where I'm desperately trying to adapt and assimilate. The way I expressed myself wasn't palatable for these new crowds. At work at a campaigning organisation, I was once told by my manager that the way I spoke scared her. I was confused, I thought I knew how to interact with people but I realised that if I felt strongly about a topic, my contribution could be mistaken as aggression. I started to think twice about what I said and how I said it. All of a sudden, communication was a minefield, like being blindfolded and stumbling my way through an unfamiliar house. This pressure to be polite and palatable was more intense as a woman of colour in a white country. And, as a *British* woman of colour, it can leave you feeling as though there's an involuntary gag in your mouth.

Known for their 'stiff upper lip' attitudes (that it is unbecoming for someone of class to express anger), Brits are more likely to adopt passive aggression in retaliation, or simply swallow it down silently. We can see this in the classic mantra 'keep calm and carry on' that came from the British Government's 1939 World War II campaign. But this wasn't always what the British demeanour was known for. In his book, *Weeping Britannia: Portrait of a Nation in Tears*, Thomas Dixon described the British around the time of Shakespeare as being known for 'sweatiness, drunkenness, meat-eating, anger, violence, simple-mindedness and melancholia.'[9] Then the French Revolution came, and while it was inspiring for its decla-ration of liberty and freedom, the revolution was also viewed by Britain as a warning sign. 'It was a moment that views coalesced around. The revolution had looked like a great triumph of humanist Republican politics, but quickly turned very nasty and very violent,' Dixon said. 'It reinforced this idea that passions were dangerous, mad and should be resisted.'[10] And so our relationship with anger became complicated and difficult.

Now we're left with a pressure to smile calmly and pretend that everything is okay, even when it clearly is not, even when we are facing the catastrophic impact of climate, technology, economic crisis to name a few. We carry on like business as usual. Like the British fear of sending something back in a restaurant, even if the dish is wrong. I call it 'White Polite'. It denies the truth in favour of keeping up appearances. It is so incongruous to how I was brought up, where if something was wrong, there wasn't hesitation to express it. Feelings, I understood, in my household, were normal and needed to be expressed. There was shouting and screaming, with both frustration and laughter. The politeness of the white class is a powerful manipulation that silences the oppressed, placing them in a trap whereby if they express dissatisfaction of norms, they are viewed as impolite, disruptive, aggressive. Politeness can be violent in this sense. Martin Luther King Jr spoke of the 'polite' racism of white liberals in 1965. In reference to the brutality experienced in the American South and the mistaken belief that racial discrimination did not exist in the North of the United States, he wrote;

'As the nation, Negro and white, trembled with outrage at police brutality in the South, police misconduct in the North was rationalized, tolerated, and usually denied. [Leaders in Northern and Western states] welcomed me to their cities, and showered praise on the heroism of Southern Negroes. Yet when the issues were joined concerning local conditions, only the language was polite; the rejection was firm and unequivocal.'[11]

When I worked in offices in the UK, in so-called cosmopolitan London, the very mention of the word 'racism' would make my (almost always) white colleagues blush. It was inappropriate to bring up racism because apparently it did not exist there. White Polite is the gagging of honesty, truth and emotion. To keep things as they are. So that the whites can stay unflustered, unblushing. The times I have taken to my hair to express myself, when I've chopped off my long hair or grown my leg and armpit hair to take a stand about my femininity, it has felt safer than speaking.

It is a special kind of anger, the one that compels you to act out on your body rather than your external environment. By cutting my hair I was able to say something to everyone around me without saying a word. I was able to say, 'I am serious, back off.' It was the human equivalent of aposematism; the signalling an animal does to warn others away and protect itself by threatening attack, like changing colours or expressing a scent. It was lashing out without putting myself at real risk.

19th century German philosopher, Friedrich Nietzsche, said 'In Christianity neither morality nor religion come into contact with reality at any point.' Reality is messy and sinful and maddening. And our learned behaviours, to suppress those things, partially because of the morality of religion that has seeped into our culture, are disconnected from that reality. The reality of the oppression faced by these women, the reality of the constraints they are under and the suffocation they feel. What if it is righteous to be angry, because without anger we don't change?

Nietzsche believed that our problem isn't that we're angry, it's that we haven't channelled our anger into the desire to change things for the better, to master anger by getting angry at the things we should be angry about, to get angry at the right things for the right reason. To master the art of anger. Aristotle's view was that passions are what allow the 'eye of the soul' to perceive moral value. I've been working in activism for the last fifteen years and often get asked how a person should choose which issues to fight for, when there are so many problems in the world. I usually tell people to think about what makes fire in their belly, what pisses them off the most. Because whatever it is that stirs up those feelings of rage, that is a signpost to what matters to you, to what your values are. It's a good indicator for where you should apply your energy and alchemise that anger into activist energy. Anger is a necessary fuel if we want anything to change.

Chapter 3
Mohawks/Rebellion

I first met Andy at a friend's house party. He had a mohawk.

'What's with the hair?' I asked.

'I'm going through a rebellious phase,' he responded.

I didn't pay much attention, an unusual hairstyle was not unexpected in that particular group of friends – misfits who had found each other in dingy pubs and warehouses in East London. We went to parties that were full of illegal drugs with Socialist Workers Party posters pasted on walls covered in unimaginative graffiti like *Your mum gives good head*. It wasn't clear if this was a political movement or a gathering of the idle. Or does every political movement start with the feeling that you're killing time? Regardless, the ingredients were there; the frustration with the way things are, people who didn't belong in the mainstream, artists, bartenders, the unemployed. The use of the body as a battlefield. Tattooed necks, pierced septums, split tongues, hairy armpits, shaved heads. Every body part had a use when it came to making a statement.

In 2014, I worked as a campaigner, attending council meetings to stop evictions and organise protests for better housing rights. David Cameron was Prime Minister and Boris Johnson Mayor of London – benefit cuts were causing deaths and increasing numbers of families were pushed out of their homes to make way for luxury developments. Andy, I learned, was an actor who made his money handing out flyers in the streets of Shoreditch. He was a Mancunian, working class boy who found himself surrounded by London's middle class arty crowd. We talked a lot about politics. He cared about his community but was the kind who might not vote. *What was the point when the same gang of toffs are always running the show?* When Thatcher died, he was part of a group who got in the news for turning their backs on her coffin as it made its way through London. In a group of imposters, he seemed to be the real thing. You could tell just by looking at him. It wasn't just his hair, it was his body too, it had something to say. He had tattoos on his arms, one of a fist clutching a red rose and another of a zig zagging line that he said was a resistor.

*

In *Everybody*, writer Olivia Laing contemplates the compulsion to manipulate one's body when it feels under threat.

> 'The victories of feminism, gay liberation and the civil rights movement overturned one by one, assuming they'd ever been secured at all… What they all shared was a desire to return the body from an object of stigma and shame into a source of solidarity and strength, capable of demanding and achieving change.'[1]

The very thing that is under threat has been used as a way to push back and exert power in the history of movements. Because when our liberties are at stake, the body is literally under siege. It is natural then, when threatened, that we return to the body, to take it back. To fight back.

This was never more apparent to me than during the COVID-19 pandemic. In the summer of 2020, after the murder of George Floyd by a police officer in Minnesota, a demonstration was quickly organised in London. A protest in that climate was against all odds; COVID lockdown rules had rendered activists at a standstill, the very act of leaving our homes was against the law. The demo was like no other. The protesters, including me, were all wearing masks, covering our noses and mouths as though we were in disguise, lending the event an air of anarchy. When we chanted we were throwing our voices, the words punching out but the source unclear. We weren't crammed together either. I'm five foot three, but wasn't squeezed or pushed like at other demonstrations I've been to. Far from the usual intensity of standing in a busy crowd, we were actively trying our best not to make contact with one another. A group of friendly activists walked around with a bottle of hand sanitiser and spare masks, squeezing liberally into the hands that stretched out before them and passing around protection to anyone that needed it. The very act of attending the demonstration had more power than before COVID, the message being sent was clear; justice for George Floyd was worth putting our bodies at risk.

The physical in activism is important. As someone who regularly advocates the benefits of digital activism in my work, I'm used to the cynicism that it's only 'real activism' when there are bodies in the street, meetings with representatives, people gathered at protests. The idea that taking action online 'doesn't count.' I disagree with that view but there is something different about the physical in activism. When we have few resources, our bodies can be the most powerful tool available to us. Putting itself in the way feels braver, more empowering because of the stakes. As our lives have grown increasingly online, a protest on the ground seems miraculous.

While I was organising protests and stunts, Andy was auditioning for dramas that would be shown after midnight on Channel 4. His parts always had substance, and so did he. I admired that he cared, when he could so easily sell out and take shitty TV adverts for more money. His work mattered but it would barely see the light of day. He was looking for meaning anywhere he could find it, and turned to tattoos as a way to express his voice. Using his own body as a canvas for activism, something seen in political movements throughout history. Punks against Thatcherism with their spiky mohawks, Black Panthers for civil rights with their afros out and proud, hippies against the war with their long hair and beards. Even as far back as the roaring '20s where we saw the birth of the flappers. Formed after World War I, when women had been relied on as a critical workforce, this new found agency set off a chain reaction. Shortly after, certain categories of women won the vote and then came birth control. Flappers were born out of this energy to break out of the societal prison women were trapped in and they chopped off their hair in protest. They could be found rebelling in bars dancing to jazz, wearing boxed dresses with short hemlines and smoking cigarettes with abandon.

All of these iconic hairstyles were created as an act against authorities and a fight for control. But when we look back at these movements the hairstyles are often minimised, referenced as fashion statements. In this retelling we lose the power, violence, beauty and aggression intended in the attention to an activist's hair.

Andy's mohawk was copied from the punks of the 1970s, which, some say, derived from Native American culture. A style specific to young, warrior men charged with protecting the tribe, the mohawk is also sometimes referred to as an iro (short for Iroquois, a confederacy of First Nations peoples) in indigenous communities. Historically the Natives' hair was plucked out rather than shaved and has a softer, natural touch, compared to the punk mohawk which was heavy and dense with product. 'Mohawk' comes from the people of the Mohawk nation, an indigenous people of North America who originally inhabited the Mohawk Valley in upstate New York.[2] There is no definitive source but some historians say the punk movement took inspiration from these communities and popularised the cut as a way to express themselves and their anger. They were anti-establishment, anti-corporation, anti-ownership and they wanted to show it. For the ultra-hardcore, there was the deathhawk, a mohawk with backcombed hair, making it five times bigger and much more prominent. 'Unlike fashion, hair is generally more of an accessible route into a trend or visual representation of the group you identify with,' said hair historian Rachael Gibson to *Vogue*. 'You might not have been able to afford a Vivienne Westwood outfit, but a Bic razor and some cheap hair dye did the same job of showing the world you are aligned with the punk movement.'[3]

When I spoke to Matthew Worley, Professor of Modern History at University of Reading, he agreed. 'You see it in punk memoirs all the time. They talk about watching the Sex Pistols and going home and cutting off their hair as the first gesture, first punk statement.' Not everyone needed the uniform but for some it was a gateway to embodying their beliefs. A lot of them were copying the style and attitude of punk poster boys the Sex Pistols and The Clash. The unlikely frontmen and their bandmates represented everything their fans' fathers were not. A young generation that didn't have a chance at finding a job because of the state of their country. This sentiment resonated not just in Britain, but throughout Europe.

The Pistols were thrust to prominence in the mid '70s as part of a line up alongside The Clash and Siouxsie and the Banshees, at the famous London 100 Club.[4] Punters filled the venue with fluorescent mohawks, dog collars, leather, and safety pins. This gig went down in punk history and was a tipping point, with these bands dominating the music scene across Europe shortly after. Johnny Lydon of the Sex Pistols was perhaps the most iconic of them all. Known as his alter ego, Johnny Rotten, he was outspoken and unruly. Their first and only album *Never Mind the Bollocks* included their famous single 'God Save the Queen', a daring mockery of the monarchy and UK's national anthem.[5]

Lydon was from a working class background and vocal about his disdain for the state and lack of opportunities for kids like him. Their message to young people was simple; we have no future and so let's fuck it all up. It was an anarchist anthem, though Lydon has since protested that he ever claimed to be an anarchist. In an interview with local paper *Ham & High*, he said 'Anarchy is mind games for the middle class'[6] and later, in a 2022 op-ed he wrote, 'Anarchy is a terrible idea. Let's get that clear. I'm not an anarchist.'[7] Despite this, Lydon inspired a movement to adopt anarchist views, acting against the peace and love of the hippie movement that came before it. Much of this energy was not just directed at the Queen and her monarchy. A few years after the Pistols' anthem came out, punk's real nemesis, Margaret Thatcher, came into power as Prime Minister. Thatcher replaced the comparatively benign Queen as punk's number one enemy with her aggressive free-market economic policies and dismantling of the social security net. The punks were going into battle with the Iron Lady. They adopted the equivalent of 19th century armour – spiked hair, leather jackets, and safety pins holding together their ripped jeans.

The disciples of punk used hair to express their feelings, to assert their aggression, transforming themselves into something intimidating (with literal spikes on their head). The US Civil Rights movement, on the other hand, saw hair being used to express their identity, activists refusing to assimilate to white standards by choosing to be natural, wearing their afro hair proudly.

The US civil rights era is when the first natural hair movement is on record, known as 'Black is Beautiful', pioneered by supporters of the Black Panther Party. One of the most iconic was activist and academic Angela Davis. In 1971, after four Black men performed an armed takeover of a courtroom, a warrant was issued for Davis following her connections with the gunmen and because she was the registered owner of the weapons used. Davis fled California before a subsequent manhunt, the FBI adding her to their Ten Most Wanted Fugitive List. Davis was plastered all over town on wanted posters, her afro taking up more of the picture than her face as she stared back, unsmiling. For most of white America, this was their first time coming across radical Black politics and seeing a woman with her afro hair out. 'I was portrayed as a conspiratorial and monstrous Communist (that is, anti-American) whose unruly natural hairdo symbolised black militancy (that is, anti-whiteness),' Davis said later. But many followed Davis's lead, including celebrities like the Jackson Five and Diana Ross, and campaigners that joined the Black Panther movement across the US.[8]

Five decades after her arrest, afros still possess the radicalism of her message. The hairstyle saw a resurgence in the 2000's with the rise of internet message boards as a place where Black women could form communities and ask each other for advice about how to manage their hair. 'Message boards were the thing before any Instagram, before any Facebook group,' Patrice Yursik, creator of Afrobella, told *Broadly*. 'We shared a lot of information [on a message board called Nappturality]. It was the first time that people were able to share their voice and to share what was working for them and get that, "Yes, girl!" validation that you weren't able to get in your day to day life.' She added, 'This was at a time when not everybody had natural hair, so you might have been dealing with some family that didn't like your hair or some people in your school who thought it was wack. This was a place where people were cheering each other on and happy for each other.' The internet became a place where these women could build up power to accept and celebrate themselves, to go back into their lives feeling stronger.

There is perhaps no hair, no body, that has been so overtly controlled and policed than that of a Black woman. Dating back to the era of slavery in the US, Africans who worked 'in the house' with their slave owner would have to wear their hair in a 'palatable' way, either with wigs or by shaping their hair to smooth out the kinks.[9] Then in 1786 there was the tignon law in Louisiana, a law enacted by the Spanish Governor of Louisiana, Esteban Rodríguez Miró, that forced Black women to wear tignon head scarves to cover their hair.[10] The law came about when the free women of the south, the southern creole and African women, would adorn gems and ribbons in their hair. They looked different to the white women, who apparently became increasingly jealous of their husbands' 'wandering eyes,' so the law was created to control the women of colour, to tame them. There are hundreds of years of control and shame and fear wrapped up in the natural hair of African women.

However, they are claiming back the power their hair embodies, with writers, activists and academics beating the drum for Black hair and the communities' right to flaunt it, speak about it and make art about it. Emma Dabiri has written extensively about the history of Black hair, including its colonisation and the subsequent systemic racism experienced by the Black community in the UK.

'As a Black child with tightly coiled hair growing up in an incredibly white, homogenous, socially conservative Ireland, I remember being told that I was "lucky I was pretty," which meant that I could "almost get away with being Black."[11]

There is now a growing movement in Europe and North America to change the policies and laws that prohibit styles like braids or afro hair in workplaces, schools and other institutions.

As Andy and I got to know each other more, I saw similarities between us. We both felt like outsiders in our worlds, he was surrounded by rich kids trying to be actors, and I was surrounded by the middle class do-gooders who chose to work in charities. I also noticed how much we both seemed preoccupied with our own hair. I would spend hours obsessively tweezing the slightest whisker on my face. He seemed oddly uncomfortable with the mohawk, and started to wear flat-caps more often. Then one day he told me that the mohawk was a coping mechanism. He had alopecia and didn't want anyone to know, so he had been doing what he could with the hair that was remaining, turning it into some kind of style. I realised that he wasn't making a statement, that I'd projected my own ideas onto him. I was doing exactly what I felt others had done to me all my life. He couldn't continue hiding it, his eyebrows were now victim . He'd had to live with this, his hair falling out and growing back in cycles, since he was nineteen. The growth phase had typically lasted years at a time and when it fell out, it would be in patches. But it was getting worse. I started to think back and connect the dots. Now it made sense, the clinging to an identity, an aesthetic. I realised that what Andy really cared about was being seen as a man, a lad. The tattoos, the Mancunian pride, it was all so important to him.

Virility is a fragile thing. Men, it seemed, are no different to women in having rules, some secret, some overt, to keep them in line with their gender identity. I now realise that most men I know are preoccupied with their hair. That we're all bound by fear and shame and pressure to be something.

In some ways, this wasn't that different to what the activists were doing. Andy was using his hair, or lack of, to survive. It's all about survival for these groups; surviving their oppression by fighting back. Andy was fighting the reality of being bald, of having his masculinity robbed from him because baldness can rock the very core of a man's sense of self. The Greek physician of the classical period, the so-called 'father of western medicine', Hippocrates, experienced balding and became obsessed with finding a cure (today, the most severe form of hair loss and baldness, when only a thin rim of hair remains at the sides and back of the head, is known as the Hippocratic wreath). At the time, he prescribed a topical solution of horseradish, opium, beetroot, spices, and pigeon droppings, one of many weird and obscure 'treatments' to cure baldness over the course of history. Others include rubbing kerosene on the head, washing hair with 'strong sage tea,' applying alcohol to the head, and using salt and white oak bark. Hippocrates was obsessed with the topic, likely because even as far back as the classical period there was pressure for a man to appear virile.

Having an excess of testosterone is likely to cause hair loss, but to lose his hair can threaten a man's masculinity. In Hippocrates's time, baldness was acceptable only amongst the philosophically inclined, the lack of hair suggested age and wisdom. Roman men did all they could to hide their receding hairlines. The sculpted portraits we find of Julius Caesar, Otho and Domitian all feature a luscious curly head of hair, signifying youth and power.

Andy finally shaved off the hair he had remaining. He let go of the mohawk and accepted the alopecia and hair loss in its entirety. The next time I saw him, he still looked proud. But it was softer, more honest. Less fragile. He gained power when he stopped fighting himself.

With a shaved head, Andy looked like the skinheads from my childhood. It was strange, the old familiar feeling of fear and tension when I saw a skinhead, it started to fade. He was not like the kids from home.

Newhall was where I met my first skinheads. I was around seven years old when we moved there from

Leicester which had spoiled me with all the multiculturalism and acceptance of Brown and Blackness. An opportunity to run a newsagent in Newhall had presented itself, for my parents to get out of factory work. Ever since they immigrated to the UK from India, they were working out ways they could make a living and thrive, despite everything that the state and country did to hold them back. With a degree in Agriculture, my dad explored further study but was met with impossible hoops he would have to jump through to get into a university as an immigrant. Inspired by others in our community, Dad borrowed the cash to rent the convenience shop.

I felt like an alien in that new place, not just because everyone looked and spoke so differently to us, but some of them treated us like intruders. Every evening a gang of kids would congregate outside, on the front drive of the store. One by one, the group grew bigger until at around 9pm every night, when my parents were locking up at the end of their fifteen hour day, a pack was formed, their restless energy palpable and aimed at whatever caught their attention. They would start the harassment asking seemingly innocuous questions that fast became vicious slurs, escalating for a reaction.

What's for dinner?
Why's David still banned?
Paki, paki, paki.

I knew to feel unsafe around the boys with shaved heads. Sometimes they thought it would be funny to pick on me or one of my sisters when they spotted us. I felt unsafe when I left our own house, in case they were out there, in case I hadn't spotted them from the window before I left.

During that time, news stories on local TV showed the British National Party marching on the streets in nearby Derby. At around ten years old, I didn't know who the BNP were, that they were a far right fascist party growing in power, but I gathered from the tone of the stories that it was a bad thing. Something to be worried about, especially for people like me. I remember feeling restless, about the physical safety of me and my family. I didn't speak to anyone about it and it didn't get brought up at school, it didn't seem important to anyone else.

Skinheads rose to prominence in public consciousness around 1970 with the rise of attacks in immigrant communities, namely Pakistani and Indian communities, and with Richard Allen's cult novel *Skinhead* where the life of sixteen-year-old Joe is ruled by clothes, beer, football and, above all, violence – violence against hippies, authority, and racial minorities. It wasn't until the late '70s that the far right began actively recruiting skinheads who had strayed to the political right, and co-opted the look as their own. And so the neo-Nazis' 'racist skinhead' was born and spread globally. According to the Southern Poverty Law Centre, since its emergence in Britain, there have been racist attacks by US skinheads throughout the '80s, '90s and early 2000s.

In November 1988, three racist skinheads in Portland, Oregon, beat an Ethiopian student named Mulugeta Seraw to death with baseball bats. In April 1999, a Mexican immigrant named Irineo Soto Aguilar was murdered in Lakeside, California, by three racist skinheads who crushed his skull with chunks of concrete. In October 2007, a racist skinhead strangled a 62-year-old gay man in Oklahoma City as a rite of passage in his gang.[12]

The list goes on. I'm not sure if the boys in our village were intentionally trying to copy the white nationalists but the mood was in the air, deep in their hostility when they sauntered into corner shops, waiting for the shop-keeper to give them hassle so they could retaliate with racist abuse, then later claim it was justified.

Skinheads weren't always associated with the far right. Kids from working class communities adopted skin-heads as part of the 'mod' aesthetic (a subculture named after the modern jazz they were into). It was true that they were disenfranchised and looking for something to believe in. And soon targeted by the National Front to join their cause.

This was how the skinhead developed a distinctive, violent image. A haircut, or rather lack of hair, can send an intense message, evoke powerful feelings. I hadn't yet learned what the connotations of the skinhead were when I encountered the kids in Newhall. I just knew to be wary of them because that image is soaked into our psyche, a symbol of the military, of army buzz cuts and uniformity, efficiency, obedience. A person with a buzz cut is a vessel for orders, wherever they might come from. In the same way that the mohawk of the native Indian symbolises the young boys who fought for their community, the skinhead and mohawk in western culture have become symbols for battle. In the 1976 Martin Scorsese film *Taxi Driver*, the main character, Travis, is an army veteran who had been dishonourably discharged from the Marines, growingly increasingly paranoid and agitated during the course of the film. He decides to assassinate the presidential candidate, Senator Palantine, and, in preparation, we see him shave his hair into a mohawk. Scorsese later said about the mohawk, 'In Saigon, if you saw a guy with his head shaved – like a little Mohawk – that usually meant that those people were ready to go into a certain Special Forces situation. You didn't even go near them. They were ready to kill.'[13]

Hair, and the lack of it, can be weaponised against us. But from the women in Iran to the British punks, we're taught by the brave and angry that we can also take that weapon and use it in our favour.

Andy removed his hair as a coping mechanism and reclamation of power. In doing so, I saw the skinhead in a new light; tender and naked. The skinhead was now somehow vulnerable in my eyes. But Andy was also fighting back. For a long time he would spend hours thinking and creating styles of hair that would disguise the truth of his condition, because the world he lived in had expectations of what a man should be. The power in a subculture is that it is able to reject society's expectations. The hippies, punks, skins, flappers and Panthers, each presented their own versions of men and women and, in doing so, created a new identity. The irony of these movements is that they begin with the aim of being seen as different, as individuals, but acceptance only comes in these communities if the correct style is adopted, and so individuality inevitably becomes conformity.

Conformity can be suffocating, especially the kind that stifled me throughout my childhood, but it doesn't have to be a bad thing if you're attempting to challenge the status quo. In that case, conforming to the style and substance of a new subculture is a necessity. To build up an army that can challenge the mainstream, with a strength in numbers. The individuality they were striving for was not as a single individual, but an individuality that breaks away from the masses.

We can still see the legacy of these armies around us today. When you walk into a bank, a restaurant, a supermarket, the person assisting you might have green hair, piercings, an afro. The fabric of our society has been coloured by them and one activist can recognise another in how they present themselves. Building power as they pass each other in the street.

Chapter 4
Salons/Community

One of my favourite childhood memories is spending summers at my cousin's house in Leicester after we'd moved to Derbyshire. We'd be dropped off by Dad for a few days then picked up what felt like months later. I can still remember being sat at my grandma's (or Ba, as we called her), feet every morning as she combed my hair and braided it into plaits. I remember vividly in those moments with my Ba, feeling so loved. She spoke Gujarati, which I understood but I was fast losing my grip on the language as I spent more time in our new, predominantly white village. Little was said between us but the comb's teeth on my scalp, through my hair was soothing, meditative.

During my childhood, Newhall had a population of less than 700, nearly all white. My community back in

Leicester, that we visited regularly, was still our real home. There, we looked alike, we ate the same food, spoke the same way, used the same coconut oil to treat our hair. It was especially exciting to go back when there was a wedding. We would turn up a day or two in advance, the kids piling into my cousin's bedroom, the women spending the days in the run up grooming themselves. I would hang around and watch the older girls painting their nails, picking out the flowers and clips they would pin in their hair, the smell of perfume and Mehndi and bleach swimming in the air for days. I longed for the day I would be allowed to join them, bleaching moustaches and soaking hair in oil. These were all things the girls at my school would never understand, my secret other world.

Hair and what we did with it, became a glue for our community in a way that nothing else really could. The closeness, the nakedness, the vulnerability in allowing ourselves to be groomed by each other. To this day, I feel a sisterhood with girlfriends when we're getting ready to go out. Squeezed into the same bathroom to share a mirror. Combing our hair, curling our lashes, tweezing our chins. There is an intimacy in that room that is so pure it's unidentifiable to the untrained eye, but feels as deep as though we are real sisters.

One of the many enlightening things that bell hooks said about community was that 'beloved community is formed not by the eradication of difference but by its affirmation, by each of us claiming the identities and cultural legacies that shape who we are and how we live in the world.'[1] It's understood most intensely by people I know of Black, Asian or Latino communities, those outside of white culture. There is an unspoken understanding that hair and the things we do with it are special and brings us closer. A sacred practice.

Campaigner Seyi Falodun-Liburd told me about growing up in North London. Her aunt taught her how to braid on her dolls and in turn Seyi taught her friends at school how to braid their own hair. The practice helped Seyi connect to her Blackness and with other girls in her school, managing a type of hair that wasn't visible in the girls magazines when she was growing up.

'As a child, hair was my first site of play and creativity. And it was also a guaranteed moment of intimacy between me and the women and other girls in my life. Whether it was my mum braiding my hair and asking me about my day, or lunchtime in secondary school when I'd braid my best friend's hair while we all talked about boys and music – I remember the bonds created between us in those moments that were at the root of our community and culture.'

Throughout her childhood Seyi, like me, didn't see herself in the culture. So while the other white girls could turn to the magazine shelves for advice as they navigated their adolescence, Seyi and her friends had to learn themselves and through community, tips and tricks being passed down through generations of Black women. They built up trust and sisterhood through lessons they couldn't teach at the convent school she attended run by white nuns, or in the way white kids might learn how to do their hair by reading *Just Seventeen*. At fourteen years old, Seyi provided the girls at her school with a lunchtime service, plaiting their hair in return for a few quid. If the nuns ever came across them they'd put a stop to it, creating a tighter bond between the girls as they were othered by the adults in their school. Those early experiences were where Seyi first experienced the intimacy and connection that came from hair. Years later, she found that she had started to lose that connection when she straightened her hair.

'When I started unlearning the harmful rhetoric around Black hair being unruly or difficult to manage, and understanding their beginnings in white supremacy I started feeling much more freedom in playing with my hair again. I didn't realise that I had stopped, my focus had become something I could easily maintain while looking "professional" as I entered the world of work. Now bantu knots, canerows and flat twists are my go-tos, "professionalism" (read: white supremacy) takes a backseat to joyful expression and comfort.'

Hair doesn't just bind communities, it's a way to express and communicate powerful, complex emotions. Shaving one's head is a sign in some Ethiopian cultures that the person is mourning someone they loved – an appropriately dramatic gesture for the more jarring experiences of the human condition. It is done in a ritual meant to help with the healing process of grief, to know that even though the person is physically gone, death has started a new form of communication between the living and dead. The shaved head is a language.

In South Africa there is a similar ritual, 'for the Xhosa, Zulu, Ndebele and Tswana cultures, the occurrence of death is something that affects the whole community not the individual or individuals concerned. It is not only one person who is bereaved but the whole community.'[2] An individual's hair doesn't represent only them, but their entire community, something done to one's own body can be healing for those they love.

Similarly, the 2022 movement of women in Iran campaigning against Islamic laws are attempting to hurt the regime they are under through communal action.

Hair can be such a bond in a community that a person acting out on their own, in order to say something, can spark a feeling, and reaction, in the community that they are bound to.

When my Ba passed away, I experienced grief and the process of mourning in a newly personal way. It was 2019 and was not unexpected, our Ba had lived a long life. We aren't sure what age she was when she passed because records weren't kept for our Indian elders as they are now. Ba was around for my entire childhood and adulthood, she had moved to the UK with my mother in the '70s. She was there when I was born and took care of me as my mum and dad worked long hours making a living for their growing family. She would plait my hair, I would give her massages, we would sleep in the same bed. I still remember her smell, her cotton sari absorbed everything and gave off a faint reminder by the end of the day. Gentle smells of turmeric and ginger. The aroma of her balm, the oil in her hair. Even her body odour was a comfort.

She was there through every significant moment for our family. She was there in Lancashire where I was a baby, with my parents as they figured out parenting and working in a strange and northern English town. When my cousin's family and ours were all living in a cramped semi-detached in Leicester, she was there, and when we moved to Derbyshire, windswept by the whiteness and hostility that came our way. She was always there and then she wasn't. Our family was floored by her death.

As Hindu tradition dictated, for thirteen days after the cremation, our family mourned. The front door was always open, friends and family came by throughout. There were tears, laughter, lots and lots of eating. A cooked Indian spread catered and ready for any hour. People came and went, but our immediate family stayed for the whole time. My uncle grew his hair and his beard. My cousin too. As the days passed, hair grew and grew, marking how long it had been since we had lost our granny. The wildness of their appearances, matching the tiredness of their weary eyes. We would sit cross legged in the front room, mattresses spread out on the floor, laughing about something silly, a memory of one of us as a kid, and mid conversation their appearance would catch my eye and I was instantly reminded why we were all there, heart panging. On the final day of mourning, for the funeral, they shaved.

I don't know if they realised it but what they did for us was a gift. Their physical display, a constant, dishevelled reminder about what had happened. It was bonding and strengthening for us all. Expectation to keep a tidy appearance was set aside and the dishevelled hair became a symbol for great sorrow, the calamity we were suffering. In Hindu scripture, there is a story about a woman called Draupadi who took an oath after she was dragged through the court by her hair and then molested by the prince Dushasana. She vowed that she would remain with dishevelled hair until it was washed in the prince's blood and she was properly avenged.[3] The dishevelled hair as a vow is made more powerful in a culture where respectability is a virtue.

Acts of tradition related to hair are not just gestures to the community but also to God. There is a practice by priests and monks called tonsure, of cutting or shaving some or all of the hair on the scalp as a sign of religious devotion or humility. They say the monks did this to be closer to God. It seems reassuring and comforting to me, the idea of treating your body as a vessel for a greater meaning. A precious, sacred canvas.

These powerful ways of creating connection with ourselves and each other are dependent on a religious belief and thousands of years of tradition, rules created by the very system that promotes patriarchy and supremacy in society. We are slowly losing connection with religion in society at large. Could it be possible to create the same kind of sacred connection without religion?

One of my favourite moments from a book is the salon scene in Chimamanda Ngozi Adichie's *Americanah*. It runs the course of several chapters, starting with the train journey to the salon, to the moment the protagonist Ifemelu leaves, and we are immersed in vivid detail throughout. With no braiding salon in white Princeton where she lives, she pilgrimages to a shop in Trenton, New Jersey. We are taken through every arduous step, from the sweltering heat, the catching of the train, the pangs of hunger, and making it to the Mecca she journeyed to. Sitting in a salon having her hair braided for six hours by ladies from French-speaking West Africa, she munches carrots and granola bars while they are eating spicy and greasy food. She reads an American novel while they stare in rapture at Nigerian Nollywood movies.[4]

The world Adichie paints in that salon is an insight into Ifemelu's growing Americanisation, but also a demonstration that the salon will always bind their Blackness. The Black salon, more than any other, is a social space, a community meeting point. The white world of America that Ifemelu occupies others the Black experience, including the unsolicited touching of Black hair. This makes the act of touching Black hair heightened, as a protected act. The Black salon becomes a space where a woman can relax, momentarily, from the whiteness of the world she experiences every day. For Taylor Bryant, writing for *NYLON* magazine, the salon is a refuge, a place to find people like you.

'There's one time in particular that makes me think of the salon as a place to be when times are bad. I was in the salon when George Zimmerman was found not guilty of murdering Trayvon Martin back in 2013. It was the only time I experienced the salon being a sombre space. But though there was disappointment in the air, there was no shock. This is just how these things pan out for us, was the unvoiced declaration of everyone there. But, in-between the silence, was also an understanding that, though the outside might not always be safe, there, in-between those four walls, we would always have a place where we are welcome.'[5]

Ain't No Time for Women is a documentary set in a Tunisian salon on the evening of the first round of the presidential elections in 2019, the second election since the collapse of the dictatorial regime of Zine El Abidine Ben Ali. As the film's opening credits explain, 'a rise in religious conservatism sparked by the arrival of the Islamic party Ennahda has revived the fighting spirit of Tunisian women.' While in the safety of each other's company, these women are free to mock the government, discuss the election and ask one another who to vote for. They take release from the tight leash of their country in the salon.

'Can you see any greys?'
'Who are you voting for? You don't know? I don't know anything anymore, there are 26 candidates.'

'Madam, Zibidi is a good man. He won't abuse power. Even my daughter's husband is voting for him.'[6]

There is freedom and power in these women, while having their hair dried and curled, washed and combed, to speak openly about tense political matters on the evening before the first vote. Significantly, there are no men present. Just like in Adichie's Black salon, there are no white people. The salon has the perfect combination of intimacy and a 'closed door' that makes it a safe haven, a place to find 'your people', to put down your guard, hang up your coat and let your hair down.

Hair historian Rachel Gibson, who has dedicated her work to writing about and working in the hair industry, told me, 'I get angry about people dismissing hair, that it's just a job for women and gay men.' She makes a good point, that despite the power of the salon, of all it can do and is capable of, the role of hairdresser gets little respect as a 'serious' job in our Western world. Growing up in the working class Midlands, I learned to believe there were two types of kids in my school; the ones who got the good grades and went to university to eventually get a 'fancy' job, and those who didn't show promise and were expected to get jobs in the area, as hairdressers or electricians. This isn't the case in other cultures where hair braiders for certain African tribes are seen as experts and revered. The person who braids hair performs it as both a ritual and a social service, an art form taught by the senior female member of the family to her daughters and close friends. As far back as Ancient Egypt, barbers were highly respected, often serving as religious priests in addition to caring for their community's hair. A salon has an extraordinary power to transform, not just our hair, but our feeling of belonging, creating a haven from the harshness of the world outside.

My Ba lived in the UK for over five decades, in a country that wasn't really her home, but the community of our family, and the extended community of our caste, helped her to feel both a sense of belonging and being taken care of. Community is a life force. It is central to the human experience, we need it to survive. Without it we feel separate, disconnected. Without community we can die. Reports of fatal loneliness have risen over the last two decades as the world has grown more connected online and less connected in our real lives. Loneliness in heart failure patients was associated with a nearly four times increased risk of death.[7] Our entire ecosystem is one giant community, plants and animals thriving from one another, getting life.

The 1994 documentary *Three Salons at the Seaside*[8] is a fly-on-the-wall look at three Blackpool hairdressing salons where an elderly community carries on its daily life oblivious to the hordes of tourists on its doorstep.

We watch as the elderly customers sit in the salon chair making idle chat that ranges from last night's dinner to remembering their lost loved ones. It seems clear that some of these women are incredibly isolated and that the trip to the salon is a way for them to have connection, perhaps the only humans they will interact with all week. Some of them visit to get their hair done every other day. Their hairdresser recognises her role in their lives and goes further than merely delivering her services, taking one of the ladies to the hospital when she has a fall. Tellingly, the lady went to her hairdresser before anyone else for help. The support, care and company that these women rely on is a lifeline.

Human beings are not made to be loners like the platypus or the fox. The platypus is so dedicated to its solitude that just a few months after laying its young, the mother will abandon it. The fox lives alone in its den, avoiding contact with any other creature. But humans need each other. To gather, to touch, to play with.

Growing up with three sisters and many cousins around meant when left to our own devices at home, we had to make our own fun. We got out makeup, hair accessories, painted our lips and filmed with our family VHS video camera. The salon recreates that feeling. Everyone is there to create and be created. A place to play. A place to spend time with a stranger who we allow to run their hands in our head, in a way only a loved one would. The massage at the sink, feeling at once taken care of and guilty for enjoying the intimate touch of a stranger.

We do less of this as we grow older, we stop playing idly with the hair of our mother or sibling. And most of us brush, plait and tidy our own hair for most of our adult lives. It's only on those occasions that we go to a hairdresser and let them take control of our hair, of us. It's only then that we get a glimpse of what it used to feel like for our hair to be played with. During the COVID pandemic when going to the hairdresser was illegal at certain times, I longed for that feeling. It is so primal that to be starved of it can make you feel strangely dissociated. Our touch and connection to one another is important in making us feel as though we are real humans. That we're alive and are cared for.

There's been a rise in discourse around the mental health of men over the last few years, with the biggest killer of men under 35 in the UK being suicide. There are now barbershops in the UK and US who train their staff to have sensitive conversations as an intervention into this epidemic. The Lions Barber Collective, founded by Tom Chapman after losing his friend to suicide, trains up barbers all over the UK, turning the salon chair into a therapist's couch. The barbershop is a space where these men can shut the door on the outside, while a stranger is tending to them, and speak openly without judgement.

In her writing on activism, bell hooks often came back to the power of community. Time and again we have learned in history that community helps humans thrive, '[O]ne of the most vital ways we sustain ourselves is by building communities of resistance, places where we know we are not alone.'[9] For a long time I thought that power had to be fought for, to be clung to or grasped at. In trying to feel at ease with my body I bleached and shaved and tweezed to conform. And then I cut my hair drastically or grew my body hair to push back. It's draining to be in constant struggle with power, in opposition to or fighting for more of it but hair can bind us, create a closeness that connects us to our communities deeply, powerfully. Making *us* powerful. Creating a power *within*.

Chapter 5
Wigs/Play

It might seem like a contradiction that being in fancy dress makes me feel more free to be myself, through masquerade, elaborate makeup, costumes and wigs. I spent a lot of my life feeling like I should be something else so I've always loved pretending. Dressing up allows me to suspend reality, surrender to fantasies. It is permission to let go of rules and invite others to do the same.

Balancing the two worlds of white and Indian culture in my youth meant that the Indian part happened behind closed doors. The brightly coloured assortment of fabrics we wore as Punjabi suits and lehengas, the grown-ups in their saris, all covered in jewels and embroidery. The bindis and arms full of bracelets and hairpieces glimmering with diamantes. None of this was seen by the kids or teachers at my Newhall school, the people that came to our shop, the people in the street where we lived. It only happened in Leicester. Leicester was different, it was where this magical world lit up in full colour.

My three sisters and I took this to another level when we played at home, often left to our own devices while Mum and Dad worked in the shop. Once the house was clear, out came the VHS camera, Mum's bag of Avon make up and the boxes of jewels emptied out the floor. We would conduct scenes from Bollywood films, my older sister always the director, my hair in a top knot and a mascara-painted moustache made me the villain. 'Main tumhen maar doonga,' I bellowed at the camera, vowing to kill the heroine, my baby sister.

When we play, we open ourselves up, become more vulnerable. We get closer to who we really are. Those two faces I put on growing up; one was tentative, hesitant and restrained for the white world I interacted with, and the other was at ease, exuberant even, when I was with my tribe of sisters and cousins playing make believe. As I grew older it was easy to lose grip of that playful part. To lose touch with the part of me that was liberated and free.

There is a long history of dress-up in the UK, heavily influenced by the European continent's indulgence in fancy dress. The Venetians were well known for their masquerade balls during the Renaissance, elaborate dances for the masked and heavily made-up upper classes, and it wasn't long before the elites of England were throwing costumed parties of their own.

'Fancy dress as a vital part of the power play and entertainment of the court was brought to life through Tudor and Stuart court masques. [Used as a] dramatic storytelling to glorify the monarch, which continued until the Civil War', writes fashion historian Amber Butchart.[1] Soon, into the 18th century, masquerade balls were opened up to anyone, beyond the monarch's court, as long as you could afford an expensive ticket. The frivolity of disguise and the play that came with it was a luxury for the elites, the parties had a hedonistic pull. There was a freedom and level of risk involved when masked, you could flirt and dance anonymously, enjoy illicit encounters that were forbidden in the light of day. This naturally prompted criticism from religious figures of the time, who condemned the act of disguise as immoral. It is perhaps not surprising that what enabled people to abandon rules, cross lines and behave so liberally became tarred as sinful.

Drag is the epitome of using dress-up to enhance and assert individuality, rather than suppress it. Drag queen Naomi Smalls, in reflecting on the hair that has inspired her wigs, said about supermodel Naomi Campbell's hair:

'There's something so striking about 30-inches-and-up, flat-ironed to the crack of your rear. Watching Naomi Campbell do a subtle neck movement that controls a sheet of glass-like shine is such a beautiful thing. Long, straight, black hair has been a staple for me since early drag due to Naomi. It's hard not to feel connected to her when wearing a long black human unit. Legs out, nose pointed to the clouds, and hips forward – she brings out a different side to Naomi Smalls that Davis [Small's birth name] doesn't have. Hair is so powerful.'[2]

The use of hair, make-up and clothing has lifted and empowered scores of drag queens and trans women, and men for decades. 'It's about survival. It's about people who have a lot of prejudices against them and who have learned to survive with wit, dignity and energy,'[3] said Jennie Livingston in reference to her documentary *Paris is Burning*. Filmed in 1986, the documentary focuses on drag queens living in New York City and their 'house' culture, which provides a sense of community and support for the flamboyant and often socially shunned performers. Groups from each house compete in elaborate balls that take cues from the world of fashion. They used this world to escape the oppressive nature of their daily lives, liberating themselves and their bodies. Some of them faced more persecution than others in the worlds they were escaping – racism was rife in '80s New York, for example – but in the Ballroom, Black men and women could rule the floor. The documentary is a window into the reality of what this group was escaping, the violence they feared in the LGBTQ community, as it's revealed at the end that one of the performers, twenty-three year-old Venus Xtravaganza, is murdered. 'It's like crossing into the looking glass, into wonderland. We go in there and feel 100% right, being gay. And it's not like that in the real world.'[4]

The first person known to describe himself as 'the queen of drag' was William Dorsey Swann, born enslaved in Maryland, US. In the 1880s, Swann hosted drag balls in Washington, DC. The parties were regularly raided by the police and eventually Swann went to prison. Most of those who attended his parties were formerly enslaved, gathering to dance in their silk dresses. The group, perhaps the first of its kind, was known as the 'House of Swann' and their parties were held in secret, invitations passed through word of mouth. Swann was arrested in police raids numerous times, including the first recorded instance of an arrest for female impersonation. Swann is one of the first activists to use their body as a battle-field. We have come a long way, partly because of what Swann and those like him did to pave the way. Centuries later, *Drag Race* placed the art of drag on the main stage, and made superstars of its performers. As *Vanity Fair* put it, *Drag Race* 'introduced – and, in turn, redefined – an entire art form to the global general public.'[5] It has taken a long and difficult time to get to this point. Power can be created by fiercely, playfully, mischievously, crossing the boundaries that are forced on us.

Binaries and rules are the opposite of play. The rules we adopt as children, for how children should look and act, they compartmentalise us. They restrain us and hold back our power. To truly liberate ourselves, we need to embrace the art of boundary breaking that is millennia old. People have been identifying as non-binary in recorded history for over 2000 years within Hindu communities. The *Kama Sutra*, dated all the way back to 400 BCE – 200 CE, mentions the performance of fellatio by 'feminine people of a third sex.'[6] This language and imagery has since been interpreted in different ways, including a reference to eunuchs, intersex and trans people. Collectively known in India as the 'third gender', there are references to them in the ancient religious epics like the Ramayana and the Mahabharata. In 2014, it was estimated that around three million third gender people live in India alone. While the third gender includes a few different groups in South Asia, the most common are the hijras. Hijras are most often born male but look and dress in traditionally feminine ways, including growing and plaiting their hair, wearing saris and bindis. They were respected and held powerful roles in society, until colonialism. When the British took over direct rule of India and absolved the British East India Company, they began to whitewash Indian society, enforcing their own beliefs and banned anything that western society viewed as 'unclean and dirty', mistreating and punishing the LGBTQ+ community.

Imperialism has created a straitjacket over cultures that appeared to be wild and uncontained. In most non-Anglo cultures around the world, hair is free and utilised in beautiful ways, including playing around with norms and creating new ways of expression. But if the British, Europeans, and Americans got involved, that wildness was slowly stamped out.

In mythology and the study of folklore and religion, a trickster is a character in a story who exhibits a great degree of intellect or secret knowledge and uses it to play tricks or otherwise disobey normal rules and defy conventional behaviour. Famous tricksters include Brer Rabbit, from an African American folktale, who uses his wit to find freedom when he tricks a fox into rescuing him from a well. And Matilda, who uses her intelligence and telekinesis to overcome her evil headmistress. As the essayist Lewis Hyde puts it, the 'trickster is a boundary-crosser.' Trickster stories have taught us about the nature of rules, who creates them and challenges us to question why they should exist. The trickster represents a fluid mind and spirit, a playful character and willingness to defy authority. The trickster keeps culture evolving.

There is a clip floating around the internet of a seventeen-year-old David 'Davy' Jones of Plaistow Grove, Bromley, otherwise known as David Bowie. It's 1964, a special *BBC Tonight* segment dedicated to the burgeoning social phenomenon of men growing out their hair. Bowie is representing the newly formed Society for the Prevention of Cruelty to Long-Haired Men, 'I think we're all fairly tolerant. But for the last two years, we've had comments like, "Darling!" and "Can I carry your handbag?" thrown at us, and I think it just has to stop now.'[7] There is an obvious air of mischief in Bowie and the five boys he's on set with. The 'society' was formed as a stunt to mock the tightly-wound conservatives Bowie was feuding with. A producer on Brit music series *Gadzooks! It's All Happening* was insistent that he trim his hair before performing on the show. This stunt got plenty of coverage but was also a sign of more to come from Bowie, who spent a career refusing to adhere to gender norms of the day, mixing and playing with whatever aesthetic pleased him, challenging the status quo. Bowie was a modern day trickster, always ahead of the game, an air of irony and the power to disrupt the rules of the day.

Unaccepted in the walls of our institutions, our schools and workplaces, the act of play, of dressing up is subversive and anti-authoritarian. But like Bowie, and the drag queens or the masked Venetians, it comes from a place of joy and fantasy. It is a power not known or understood by the rule makers and oppressors. Playing with hair can create a power that is beyond their boundaries. There is no greater line of defence and attack than creating our own worlds, breaking existing rules and creating our own. It is the embodiment of the trickster that runs rings around the so-called powerful.

Conclusion

I'm stood in front of a mirror in my bathroom and staring at the strand of white hair that has inserted itself boldly into my life, at the age of thirty-eight. It is thick, bright white (*not* grey). It is wiry, not like my usual delicate, silky dark strands. It's proudly erect on my parting, making no effort to assimilate. I'm still battling the shame and doubts about my hair that make me police myself. I still feel I need to shave or wax certain parts. I still want to be palatable according to a standard that's been imposed on me. Doing the job of our postmodern, capitalist, supremacist society by constraining myself, changing myself, reaching for an impossible ideal.

In *Discipline and Punishment*, Foucault compares explicit, public assertions of power in society, like a public hanging, to power that happens privately. The private assertions are the institutions, the schools, prisons and workplaces where there is a more insidious, harder to define, harder to detect type of power being wielded. Where we follow rules and engage in systems that we accept without question. We become 'docile bodies'. He writes about the panopticon, a type of prison designed in the 18th century, a central observation tower placed within a circle of prison cells. From the tower, a guard can see every cell and inmate but the inmates can't see into the tower. Prisoners will never know whether or not they are being watched, which creates an illusion of always being watched and puts them constantly on best behaviour. The prisoners imprison themselves.

Our minds are the panopticon. We don't see *all* of the ways we are each abiding by rules and norms that are holding us back. We have internalised many of them and are complicit in our own oppression. Complicity in contorting ourselves to be accepted. Complicit in judging ourselves and each other if expectations aren't met. It's too ingrained in the fabric of our society and systems that have been around for thousands of years, impossible to see it all.

I've explored some of that in these pages, but really that is just the tip of the iceberg. I could write for pages about the billion dollar industry that has made a lot of old white men and one or two women very, very rich.[1] Or how our binary ideas of what men and women should do and how they should be is based on relatively recent history, and when you start to peel back a century or two, you see how much more fluid and progressive we were. How free we could be today.

Because, really, this isn't about hair. It's about how we are perceived. It's about our identities and who gets to set a standard and who is forced to follow. It starts with children, who are immediately conditioned to adopt rules, and learn to view the world with a particular, narrow lens. And then, for some of us, particularly those of us on the margins, that complicity can start to feel intensely oppressive. It can erase our identity and leave us as shadows of what we could be. It can push us to breaking point. An anger so raw that we use our bodies to express it.

That anger is a source of power. It can be mobilised and turned into movements. We need these movements, they're essential in changing our norms and creating a world where we can be ourselves, where we can be free. And the secret is that we don't have to keep draining our individual power to get that change, constantly fighting to be seen and heard. We can build power through communities, on our own terms. Through mischief and play, through finding our people, creating our own spaces and making our own rules.

While I see those white hairs in my mirror and feel discomfort, I'm also intrigued. Hair is, and always will be, my muse. I'm fascinated that this part of my body continues to speak to me and teach me things about myself. That those white hairs are now appearing in curious places, like my eyebrows and my moustache. My hair *is* me and as I grow to accept every part of myself, my hair will continue to challenge and push me in ways I sometimes resist.

I've always been drawn to the story of Samson in the Bible. Samson was one of the Nazarite judges who ruled over Israel before the time of the kings, in the Book of Judges. His story is peppered across art and culture. Samson was gifted by God with incredible strength, but if he cut his long hair, his strength would be gone. His lover Delilah betrays him and arranges his hair to be cut by the Philistines, his enemies. But it grows back and he regains his strength. In the end Samson kills himself, as well as his enemies, with his own strength;

> 'And Samson said, "Let me die with the Philistines." Then he bowed with all his strength, and the house fell upon the lords and upon all the people who were in it. So the dead whom he killed at his death were more than those whom he had killed during his life.'[2]

He was defeated by the power that his own hair gave him. I felt a bit like that, that I didn't realise the power of my hair, that it had been wielded against me for so long.

Power isn't inherently bad, it depends on how we use it. We can treat it as being something to build, within and between us, rather than creating it in opposition. The power we build in our communities, in the salons and with people 'like us', with whom we can create an intimacy, a language that is ours. The power to express ourselves, by cutting off our hair, to scream and shout when we can't do it with our voice. The power to style ourselves as other, to push against the status quo, have a mohawk or an undercut and tell the world that we're not like you, that we want things to change.

Endnotes

Prologue

1. Susan Sontag, *As Consciousness Is Harnessed to Flesh: Journals and Notebooks, 1964-1980*. Picador, 2013.

Introduction

1. Michel Foucault, Paul Robinow, *The Foucault Reader*. Penguin Books, 1991.
2. Michel de Montaigne, *The Essays: A Selection*. Penguin Classics, 1994.

Chapter 1: Blondes/Conformity

1. Phillipa Perry, *The Book You Wish Your Parents Had Read and Your Children Will Be Glad That You Did*. Penguin, 2019.
2. "Native American boy pulled from class over Mohawk haircut." Lindsey Bever, *The Washington Post*. 19 September 2015. washingtonpost.com/news/morning-mix/wp/2015/09/19/native-american-boy-pulled-from-class-over-mohawk-haircut/. Accessed 10 February 2023.
3. "S.J.Res.14 - A joint resolution to acknowledge a long history of official depredations and ill-conceived policies by the Fed-

eral Government regarding Indian tribes and offer an apology to all Native Peoples on behalf of the United States." *congress. gov*. congress.gov/bill/111th-congress/senate-joint-resolution/14. Accessed 10 February 2023.

4. Levine, S. (2003). Psychological and social aspects of resilience: a synthesis of risks and resources. Dialogues in Clinical Neuroscience. 5(3), 273-280. DOI: 10.31887/ DCNS.2003.5.3/slevine.

5. "Native American boy pulled from class over Mohawk haircut." Lindsey Bever, *The Washington Post*. 19 September 2015. washingtonpost.com/news/morning-mix/wp/2015/09/19/ native-american-boy-pulled-from-class-over-mohawk-haircut/. Accessed 10 February 2023.

6. Afsaneh Najmabadi, *Women with Mustaches and Men without Beards*. University of California Press, 2005.

Chapter 2: Buzz Cuts/Anger

1. "Wear and Appearance of Army Uniforms and Insignia." Army Regulation 670-1, 2021. upload.wikimedia.org/ wikipedia/commons/c/cd/ARN30302-AR_670-1-000-WEB-1%281%29.pdf. Accessed 10 February 2023.

2. Lee Salisbury, "Britney at Breaking Point." Waddell Media & Channel 5, 2019.

3. The New King James Version, Psalm 37:8.

4. Psalm 86:15.

5. Seneca, *On Anger: De Ira*. Translated by Aubrey Stewart. Independently published, 2017.

6. "Why Iranian women are burning their hijabs after the death of Mahsa Amini." Bill Chappell & Joe Hernandez. *NPR*, 21 September 2022. npr.org/2022/09/21/1124237272/mahsa-amini-iran-women-protest-hijab-morality-police. Accessed 10 February 2023.

7. "Grief, protest and power: Why Iranian women are cutting their hair." Celine Alkhaldi & Nadeen Ebrahim. *CNN*, 28

September 2022. cnn.com/2022/09/28/middleeast/iran-hair-cutting-mime-intl. Accessed 10 February 2023.

8. Soraya Chemaly, *Rage Becomes Her: The Power of Women's Anger*. Atria Books, 2018.

9. Thomas Dixon, *Weeping Britannia: Portrait of a Nation in Tears*. Oxford University Press, 2017.

10. Ibid.

11. 'Martin Luther King and the 'polite' racism of white liberals.' Jeanne Theoharis, *The Washington Post*, 17 January 2020. washingtonpost.com/nation/2020/01/17/martin-luther-king-polite-racism-white-liberals/. Accessed 10 February 2023.

Chapter 3: Mohawks/Rebellion

1. Olivia Laing, *Everybody: A Book about Freedom*. WW Norton, 2021.

2. "Culture and History." *Saint Regis Mohawk Tribe*. srmt-nsn.gov/culture_and_history. Accessed 10 February 2023.

3. "How protest hair became a form of political expression." Ellen Burney. *Vogue Australia*, 28 October 2019. vogue.com.au/hair-insider/how-protest-hair-became-a-form-of-political-expression/image-gallery/7749adee0c448549461b22289b0f0353. Accessed 10 February 2023.

4. "The '100 Club Punk Special': 45 years on from the stage inception of punk." Arun Starkey. *Far Out Magazine*, 2021.

5. John Lydon & Keith Zimmerman, *Rotten: No Irish, No Blacks, No Dogs*. Picador, 2008.

6. "An anarchist? I never was. Whoever told you that?" Rhiannon Edwards. *Ham & High*, 2012.

7. "John Lydon: I've no animosity against any of the royal family." Nick McGrah. *The Times*, 1 June 2022. thetimes.co.uk/article/john-lydon-ive-no-animosity-against-any-of-the-royal-family-wq55zl38h. Accessed 10 February 2023.

8. "the radical politics behind afros." André-Naquian Wheeler.

i-D, 7 July 2017. i-d.vice.com/en/article/zmn454/the-radical-politics-behind-afros. Accessed 10 February 2023.

9. "How Natural Black Hair at Work Became a Civil Rights Issue." Chanté Griffin. *JSTOR Daily*, 3 July 2019. daily.jstor.org/how-natural-black-hair-at-work-became-a-civil-rights-issue/. Accessed 10 February 2023.

10. "The Tignon Laws Set The Precedent For The Appropriation and Misconception Around Black Hair." Samantha Callender. *Essence*, 24 October 2020. essence.com/hair/tignon-laws-cultural-appropriation-black-natural-hair/. Accessed 10 February 2023.

11. Emma Dabiri, *Twisted: The Tangled History of Black Hair Culture*. Harper Perennial, 2020.

12. "Racist Skinhead." *Southern Poverty Law Centre*. splcenter.org/fighting-hate/extremist-files/ideology/racist-skinhead. Accessed 10 February 2023.

13. Andrew J Rausch, *The Films of Martin Scorsese and Robert De Niro*. Scarecrow Press, 2010.

Chapter 4: Salons/Community

1. bell hooks, *Killing Rage: Ending Racism*. Henry Holt and Company, 1996.

2. Sibongile Ndileka Yawa, *A Psycho-analysis of Bereavement in Xhosa, Zulu and Tswana Cultures*. University of South Africa, 2010.

3. N.V.R. Krishnamacharya, *The Mahabharata*. Tirumala Tirupati Devasthanams, 1983.

4. Chimamanda Ngozi Adichie, *Americanah*. Knopf Doubleday Publishing Group, 2014.

5. "An Ode to the Black Salon." Taylor Bryant. *NYLON*, 27 February 2018. www.nylon.com/articles/losing-black-hair-salon-culture. Accessed 10 February 2023.

6. Sarra El Abedd, *Ain't no Time For Women*. 2021.

7. "Loneliness and Social Isolation Linked to Serious Health Conditions." *CDC*, 29 April 2021. cdc.gov/aging/publications/features/lonely-older-adults.html. Accessed 10 February 2023.

8. Philippa Lowthorpe, *Three Salons at the Seaside*. BBC, 1994.
9. bell hooks, *Yearning: Race, Gender, and Cultural Politics*. Routledge, 2014.

Chapter 5: Wigs/Play

1. "History of Costume in England." Amber Butchart, *English Heritage*. english-heritage.org.uk/visit/inspire-me/history-of-costume-in-england/. Accessed 10 February 2023.
2. "3 Black Drag Queens Reveal Their Ultimate Hair Muses." Kayla Greaves, *InStyle*. 1 June 2021. instyle.com/hair/all-natural/black-drag-queens-hair-muses. Accessed 10 February 2023.
3. "Director Says Paris Isn't Just Dance Film." Barry Koltnow, *Orlando Sentinel*, 3 September 1991. orlandosentinel.com/news/os-xpm-1991-09-04-9109010113-story.html. Accessed 10 February 2023.
4. Jennie Livingston, *Paris is Burning*. Art Matters Inc., 1990.
5. "There Has Never Been a Show Like *RuPaul's Drag Race*." David Canfield, *Vanity Fair*. 27 August 2021. vanityfair.com/hollywood/2021/08/awards-insider-rupauls-drag-race-emmy-impact. Accessed 10 February 2023.
6. Amara Das Wilhelm, *Tritiya-Prakriti: People of the Third Sex: Understanding Homosexuality, Transgender Identity and Intersex Conditions Through Hinduism*. Xlibris, 2008.
7. "David Bowie • BBC Tonight Programme • 1964." Ziggy Stardust, *YouTube*. 6 August 2021. youtube.com/watch?v=5W38suFC0Ow. Accessed 10 February 2023.

Conclusion

1. "The 20 richest billionaires and fashion and beauty." Angelica Xidias, *Vogue Australia*. 8 March 2019. vogue.com.au/beauty/news/the-20-richest-billionaires-in-fashion-and-beauty/image-gallery/ad39e41cddff65580e6422be76d6828d. Accessed 10 February 2023.
2. The Book of Judges 16:30

Acknowledgements

I want to start by saying a huge thank you to Laura Jones and Heather McDaid at 404 Ink for giving this book a shot, and for your patience while I tried to unravel my thoughts and make sense of hair. Thank you also to Maddy Belton and Jane Graham-Maw at Graham Maw Christie agency, who initially gave me the confidence to pursue the idea of hair and power and put time into thinking it through with me. I couldn't have got here without your help at that early stage when the idea was just a seed.

I am enormously grateful to the people who spoke to me, offering me their precious stories and insights. For the expertise I especially want to thank Matthew Worley (for one of the best conversations I had in this process, talking about the punk scene and getting equally passionate about this topic) and Rachel Gibson (you need to write a book because your brain is a walking hair encyclopaedia. Thank you for lending it to me). For the stories and feedback thank you to Seyi Falodun-Liburd, Jack Graham, Suzi Siegel, Thom Carter, Guppi Bola, Chaitanya Kumar and Penny East. This book is infinitely better because of you, I owe you all drinks.

Thank you to my mum and dad who have shaped the way I see the world. And my sisters, my co-stars in this book, and such an important part of my early experiences with hair. I'm glad we went through it together. I love you guys.

About the Author

Kajal Odedra is an author and activist based in London and New York. She has over 15 years experience in activism, supporting some of the biggest people powered campaigns in the UK and around the world. She studied an MA in Creative and Life Writing at Goldsmiths University where she was shortlisted for the Pat Kavanagh Award. Her writing has appeared in the *Guardian*, *Independent*, *New Statesman* and *The Times*. Her first book, *Do Something; Activism for Everyone*, was published by Hodder in 2019.

About the Inklings series

This book is part of 404 Ink's Inkling series which presents big ideas in pocket-sized books.

They are all available at 404ink.com/shop.

If you enjoyed this book, you may also enjoy these titles in the series:

Sons and Others: *On Loving Male Survivors* – Tanaka Mhishi

Sons and Others challenges misconceptions and misrepresentations of sexual violence against men across media and society and offers a new way of seeing and understanding these men in our lives, asking how the violence they experience affects us all.

BFFs: The Radical Potential of Female Friendship
– Anahit Behrooz

Friendships can be the foundation of early memories and formative moments. But why are they seen as secondary to romantic, or familial connection, something to age out of? *BFFs* is an examination of the power of female friendship, not as something lesser, but as a site of radical intimacy, as told through the cultural touchstones around us.

No Man's Land: Living Between Two Cultures
– Anne East

In *No Man's Land*, Anne East explores the chasm of living between two cultures, how it is to feel one thing and yet be perceived as another, the emotions felt within this limbo, and why culture truly matters. More so, she considers how this has manifested through history, and the British Empire, with focus on the often unheard or ignored impacts on those of East and Southeast Asian heritage.